Chatham Dockyard

IN OLD PHOTOGRAPHS

Chatham Dockyard, Main Gate. Built in 1720, the main gate to the dockyard is a three-storey brick building that has served as one of the town's major landmarks for over 250 years. This particular photograph shows the gate some time before the First World War. Dockyard workers are entering the gate, ready to begin a further stint of work.

Chatham Dockyard

IN OLD PHOTOGRAPHS

PHILIP MACDOUGALL

A Budding Book

First published in 1994 by Alan Sutton Publishing Limited

This edition published in 1998 by Budding Books, an imprint of Sutton Publishing Limited
Phoenix Mill · Thrupp · Stroud · Gloucestershire
GL5 2BU

A catalogue record for this book is available from the British Library

ISBN 1-84015-038-6

Typesetting and origination by
Sutton Publishing Limited.
Printed in Great Britain by
WBC Limited, Bridgend, Mid-Glamorgan.

Contents

The ironclad battleship, *Bellerophon*. Launched at Chatham in 1865, she is seen here in No. 2 dock for the purpose of having her hull cleaned. Almost certainly, the photograph dates to the year 1873 when *Bellerophon* was being prepared for service abroad. The picture provides an excellent view of the various steam cranes and horse-drawn carts that were so much a feature of the yard at this time.

Introduction

Chatham Dockyard can date its origin to the year 1547. In that year a building was rented for the storage of rigging and sails belonging to the royal ships then wintering in the Medway. In 1570 the dockyard itself was born, when a mast pond was completed. During the following year land for storehouses, a forge and other dockyard buildings were acquired. This land, the site of the original dockyard, was to the south of the historic dockyard. Most of the work undertaken at Chatham in these early years was connected with the maintenance and repair of royal ships. In 1586 though, orders were given for the construction of a 40-ton pinnace. Named *Sunne*, this was the first vessel constructed at Chatham.

Considerable expansion of the yard occurred in the following century. It was then that the dockyard moved to its present site, with the original Elizabethan yard finally turned over to the unloading and storage of guns. By 1699 Chatham Dockyard covered 68 acres and included three single docks, a double dock and building slip. Supplying permanent employment for more than nine hundred workmen, it was the largest civilian employer in the country.

The importance of Chatham during the seventeenth century cannot be overstated. With the Dutch as the nation's main adversary, the yard was particularly well placed. Ships at anchor in the Medway could, with a minimum of delay, take offensive action against the Dutch, while remaining well placed to protect those areas most likely to be attacked. All this, of course, assumed a degree of readiness on the part of the Navy – and this was not the case in 1667. In that year the Dutch, having devised a masterly plan, simply sailed a squadron of ships into the Medway and inflicted the most embarrassing naval defeat ever suffered by this country.

It was towards the end of the seventeenth century that Portsmouth began to supersede Chatham as the country's premier naval dockyard. The Medway's once deep waters had begun to shoal, and the French replacing the Dutch as a major enemy meant that Portsmouth gained greater strategic value. Chatham became neglected and fewer ships were sent there for refitting. This situation did not affect the construction of new ships, and during the eighteenth century many notable ships were built at Chatham.

Only during the 1850s was this long period of neglect terminated. At this time considerable areas of marshland were reclaimed for dockyard expansion, and work started on three enclosed basins running along the line of St Mary's Creek together with four new dry docks (with a fifth added later in the century) and a great variety of workshops, factory buildings and storehouses. It is this period of the yard's history that marks the opening section of this book. Surprising as it may seem, there are a considerable number of photographs from these very early years. Taken by members of the Royal Engineers, they show various aspects of the work that had to be undertaken during the building of the Victorian extension.

The late nineteenth century was perhaps the busiest period in Chatham's long history. From 1860 onwards, Chatham was launching, on average, two new ships every year. Among the largest of these were three battleships of the 'Majestic' class – *Illustrious*, *Magnificent* and *Victorious*. Completed during the mid-1890s, they displaced 14,900 tons and were to remain in service throughout the First World War.

The arrival of the twentieth century brought a completely new skill to Chatham – that of submarine building. The first, *C.17*, was launched at Chatham in 1908. Having proved its ability to build submarines, numerous orders were now placed at Chatham for additional craft. By 1914 the dockyard had gained further experience with the construction of both 'D'- and 'E'-class submarines. But it was the First World War that really sealed the submarine connection. During those four fateful years fifteen vessels were launched at Chatham, of which all but three were submarines.

The cessation of hostilities saw a number of uncompleted submarines scrapped, with a period of five years elapsing before any further vessels were launched. The first of these new craft was *X-1*, a submarine that was far in advance of her day. Designed as an underwater cruiser she had, in addition to six torpedo tubes, four 5.2-in guns which enabled her to engage hostile shipping on the surface. The only one of her class, she was not really a success, being too slow, while her advanced design generated an endless series of problems.

With the approach of the Second World War the pace of work once again increased. Construction of 'S'-class submarines was the dockyard's primary role, with eight of this type launched in the immediate pre-war years. Between 1940 and 1945 a number of 'Porpoise' and 'T'-class submarines were also built. As can be imagined, the wartime period was particularly busy, with 1,360 refits undertaken together with sixteen new launchings.

During the post-war years submarines continued to be built at Chatham, with *Oberon*, *Ocelot*, and *Onslaught* constructed for the Royal Navy. In addition, three Canadian 'Oberons', *Ojibwa*, *Onondaga* and *Okanagan*, were also built at Chatham.

Following closely on the launch of the last 'Oberon', work started on a £4 million nuclear submarine refit complex. Opened in 1968 it supposedly gave Chatham a secure future, designed to refit and fuel the Royal Navy's 'Fleet' class submarines. Included within the complex were two re-utilized dry docks, a refuelling crane, offices, workshops and a health physics building.

Despite the belief that, with the construction of these nuclear facilities, Chatham Dockyard had a secure future, things did not work out as hoped. A severe pruning of the nation's defence budget led to an announcement in June 1981 that the yard would be closed. Although the decision was bitterly contested by local trade unionists, the government proved unrepentant, putting a three-year rundown programme into immediate effect. To help alleviate local difficulties, several projects were put into operation, with the dockyard divided into three separate areas. Part of the former dockyard was subsequently developed as a commercial port while a second and larger area was completely redeveloped for the accommodation of housing and offices. Finally, the original historic end of the yard was handed over to a trust that had as its given objective the creation of a living museum.

SECTION ONE

The Victorian Dockyard

One of the largest civil engineering works ever undertaken in south-east England was that of a massive extension to Chatham Dockyard. Constructed between 1862 and 1885 it more than quadrupled the area previously occupied by this ancient naval yard. The new facilities included four dry docks, factory buildings, hydraulic capstans and numerous steam cranes. The centrepiece was three interlinked basins running the length of the former St Mary's Creek and designed for receiving warships. The largest of these basins, encompassing 28 acres, was for refitting work, while the other two, of 20 and 21 acres, were for completion and repair work. Undertaking much of the construction work were hundreds of convicts whose sentence of hard labour had brought them to a purpose-built prison that adjoined the yard. Among tasks they undertook were those of brick-making, simple construction work and the digging of foundations for various buildings.

An unusual aspect of the extension, bearing in mind that it was built during the mid- to late nineteenth century, was that progress was photographically recorded. Responsible for this were members of the Corps of Royal Engineers who were based at Brompton. The important military implications of the camera had been recognized, so these photographs were primarily taken for experimental purposes. That they also recorded an important piece of social history is a fortunate coincidence.

Chatham Dockyard during the mid-nineteenth century. Steam power was becoming increasingly important both for the building of ships and the means by which they were powered. Lying alongside the dockyard wall is a recently completed wooden paddle sloop, while the vessel in dry dock is a timber-hulled steam and sail warship. In truth, these two vessels merely represent a period of transition. Eventually, the dockyard would not only dispense with all forms of sail and paddle power but would build warships constructed entirely of iron. Among other features seen in this engraving are various docks and covered slips, together with a pump house and the chimneys that belong to various workshops. Particularly noteworthy are the slip coverings to the right. Still in existence, they are in the care of the Chatham Historic Dockyard Trust and consequently open to public viewing.

A detailed view of the No. 2 dock as it appeared in 1858. Having just been lengthened and rebuilt in stone it was about to play an important role in the future of the yard. In August 1861, *Achilles*, the first ironclad battleship to be built in a royal dockyard, was laid down in this dock.

A further view of the No. 2 dock. The vessel under construction is the ironclad battleship, *Achilles*.

Achilles under construction in No. 2 dock. Almost certainly this photograph was taken in February 1862, with work on the vessel's frames well in hand. To the left can be seen part of the covered workshop which had been erected over the adjoining No. 1 dock. It contained numerous machines for the cutting, bending and slotting of the armoured plates that would eventually give *Achilles* protection while at sea. Beyond the No. 2 dock *Defence* has just arrived off the dockyard. She is a further ironclad battleship. Recently commissioned into the Channel Fleet, *Defence* was the latest product of the commercial yards, having been launched the previous year. As for *Achilles*, her importance for the dockyard at Chatham cannot be overestimated. Prior to her construction, Chatham had been involved only in the building of timber ships. This was in marked contrast to the private building yards which had been making steady advances in iron. As a result, with the future of shipbuilding undergoing revolutionary change, thought had been given to the possible closure of Chatham and most of the other naval dockyards. All work, especially when it involved iron shipbuilding, would be transferred to the private yards. The Admiralty, far from happy with such a suggestion, decided that a single iron battleship should be built in one of the naval dockyards as an experiment. The yard chosen was Chatham, and the ship laid down was *Achilles*. Although numerous problems had to be confronted, not least the retraining of the workforce, the experiment proved a success. The new vessel was completed in forty-two months (private yards often took longer) and a considerable financial saving was made. (Royal Engineers Library)

Work on *Achilles* continues. This *Illustrated London News* engraving was published in April 1862 with the vessel now twenty months from her launch. The stem, which had been supplied by the Thames Iron and Shipbuilding Company, has been positioned and secured. The *Illustrated London News* described the stem as 'a splendid specimen of iron forging'.

Achilles shortly after her launch from No. 2 dock. She is seen moored off Gillingham with a number of dockyard barges lying alongside. Almost certainly they are delivering the armament for the upper and lower decks. In achieving the success of building *Achilles* in such a short time, thoughts given to the possible closure of Chatham yard were not only terminated but agreement was given to a long-delayed scheme to extend the yard to St Mary's Creek and the nearby island of St Mary's. Furthermore, Chatham was to take a leading role in the construction of future ironclads, with the first of any new class to be laid down in the dockyard. (Royal Engineers Library)

Convicts at work on St Mary's Island. Much of the dockyard extension was the product of prison labour. Placed under armed guard, gangs of convicts were marched from the prison to their place of work and instructed to carry out the many necessary tasks for construction of the enlarged shipbuilding and repair yard. The island occupied most of their attention as, prior to any construction work, it had to be protected from flooding during very high tides. For this purpose, a dam had to be built at each end of St Mary's Creek; a retaining wall was also necessary. Because of the unsuitability of the ground, the foundations of this wall had to be set on piles driven 60 ft into the ground. Once the island had been secured, work could begin on various buildings together with the three enclosed warship basins. The use of prison labour at Chatham, greatly expanded during the late nineteenth century, had been a feature of the yard for most of the century. Apart from the extension works, convicts had been used in the original part of the yard where they had been involved in the construction and improvement of dry docks.

Prison guardhouse from a late nineteenth-century engraving. Situated close to the former Alexandra Gate, the prison guardhouse serves as proof that convict work parties were once employed in the older part of the dockyard. At the top of this building can be seen an observation tower, used by prison warders to keep a watch on prisoners employed on general labouring duties.

A view across the northern end of the dockyard, *c.* 1865. In the foreground is the original wall of the dockyard; beyond is the area earmarked for the dockyard extension. Apart from the damming of St Mary's Creek, little additional work appears to have been undertaken. (Royal Engineers Library)

The austere and very bleak entrance to Chatham Prison. Built during the 1850s, it housed some of the worst offenders of the age. Prior to its construction, those convicts employed at Chatham were housed in hulks moored in the River Medway. (Royal Engineers Library)

The prison governor's house, *c.* 1857. This lay just outside the prison and provided accommodation for the governor and his family. (Royal Engineers Library)

The coffer dam at the mouth of St Mary's Creek. This was one of the earliest tasks undertaken by the convicts building the extension. The dam prevented water flowing into the creek and allowed work to begin on the three interlocking basins. (Royal Engineers Library)

Pile drivers on St Mary's Island. For the purpose of securing adequate foundations it was necessary to employ a vast number of these. They drove huge timber piles deep into the soft marshy soil of St Mary's Island. (Royal Engineers Library)

A further view of the St Mary's Island works. Here, convict labour appears to be constructing a retaining wall belonging to one of the basins. (Royal Engineers Library)

A small steam engine used for shifting building materials around St Mary's Island. Many such engines were used in this way, with one of them carrying the not inappropriate name *Busy Bee*. (Royal Engineers Library)

Brick hacks on St Mary's Island. Most of the bricks used in the extension of Chatham Dockyard were manufactured by convicts who worked in a brick-works located at the north end of the island. It is estimated that 110 million bricks were made on this site. (Royal Engineers Library)

The steam collier dock, 1883. Located on the south-east side of St Mary's Creek it was, at that time, in constant use for the reception of barges employed in the conveyance of materials needed for the building of the extension. (Royal Engineers Library)

Convicts, together with an armed warder, unload one of the barges using the collier dock. Possibly the cargo, on this occasion, is clay which has been brought to the yard for use in the brickfield. (Royal Engineers Library)

The repairing basin, 1868. This engraving, which appeared in the *Illustrated London News* in September of that year, shows a hive of activity. Hundreds of convicts are engaged in digging out both the basin and two of the docks. The large building in the background is Chatham Prison. The article which accompanied this illustration explained how the various basins were to be used. Warships needing repair would first enter the fitting-out basin (later known as the No. 3 basin) where the vessel would be stripped of her spars and gear before transferring to the factory (or No. 2) basin. Here, the vessel would be overhauled, and if necessary, her engines and boilers removed. She would then enter the repairing (or No. 1) basin where any defects would be made good. With this work complete, the vessel would re-enter the factory basin where she would receive her repaired machinery. Finally, re-entering the fitting-out basin she would be prepared for sea service.

The repairing (or No. 1) basin in 1871. The position taken by the engraver is more or less the same as that in the previous illustration. In the foreground is No. 5 dock with Nos 6, 7 and 8 docks also to be seen. Again, a view of the prison may be noted. In the foreground, work is proceeding on the basin wharf.

The lock pumping station soon after completion. This was one of the many buildings completed by convict labour. (Royal Engineers Library)

The battleship *Invincible* undergoing repairs in No. 5 dock. She was the first ship to make use of the new facilities at Chatham, entering the dock in June 1871. The other two basins had not yet been completed, and work on the entire extension would not be finished until 1885. (Royal Engineers Library)

SECTION TWO

A Tour of the Yard

It is November 1906. To give a better idea of what the yard was like at that time I have organized a tour. We are to meet early in the morning at Pembroke Gate. Once inside the dockyard we will walk along Pembroke Road until we get to the first of the three basins – all of them now complete. What a change has come to this area. With the Gillingham extension now in use, the convicts have all left and their prison has been demolished to make way for a naval barracks. Our tour of the dockyard will not simply be restricted to the newer parts of the yard, it will also take in the original portion of the yard normally entered through Main Gate. This area, first laid down during the reign of James I, is where most of the ships are built. Covered slipways and numerous storehouses, together with a huge ropery, are the main feature of this part of the yard. However, none of these buildings date back to the early seventeenth century; most of them are mid-Georgian or slightly later.

Anyway, it is time to begin our tour. Already I can hear the dockyard bell ringing. The chimes are warning any late-comers that they must enter the yard or they will lose a half-day's pay.

Pembroke Gate. Before passing into the yard it is necessary to have our passes checked by the police standing guard at the gate. They wear the familiar uniform of the Metropolitan Police. In fact, they are members of the Dockyard Division, a section of the Metropolitan Police that was created in 1860. They have responsibility for the security of all civilian naval yards in Britain. Their duties not only include standing watch at the gate but also carrying out regular patrols within the yard. If necessary, they have the right to stop and search all those they suspect of carrying illicit materials into the yard or of removing government property. The slightly obscured notice, just behind the constable to the right, indicates that matches must not be brought into the yard. These are to be handed over at the police office.

Having entered through Pembroke Gate we find a mass of workers ahead of us, congregating around one of the muster stations. These were conveniently positioned around the yard, with those employed in the yard having to collect a token before they could go on to their work station. These tokens had to be placed against their name, so indicating that they had arrived for work on time. Those who were late were not allowed to begin work that morning; instead they would have to return to the muster station later in the day and would then be permitted to work in the afternoon. Work hours at the dockyard were from 7 a.m. (7.30 a.m. mid-winter) until 5.30 p.m. (4 p.m. mid-winter) with a lunch break from 12 noon until 1.30 p.m. On Saturdays however, all work ceased at 12.30.

Passing along the line of docks and basins we first head to the east end of the yard. The object of this part of the excursion is to take a look at the collier wharf. Used during the last century by convicts unloading items needed for the building of the extension, it now has a more general use. Most of the vessels entering this dock are coal-ships. Each year they bring into the yard the thousands of tons of black gold that are required to keep the nation's warships either at sea or on stand-by. But today it is the turn of a timber ship to enter the collier dock. As we stand back and watch we see a huge fir timber being unloaded by the mobile crane positioned alongside the dock.

On board the general cargo ship that has brought today's supply of timber. A stevedore chargehand oversees delivery. Beyond can be seen the yard coal depot together with a hopper and various coal trucks. The general date of this (and the previous illustration) is slightly later than the suggested date for this imaginary tour of the yard. The piece of timber shown was the longest known to have been brought into the yard and was probably required to fulfil a special task (possibly designated as a mast for a naval base). As for the stevedore chargehand, this was Mr Butter. It was his daughter, Mrs Ainsworth, who loaned me these two photographs. She informs me that her father was born in 1891 – clear proof, if more were needed, that I've cheated slightly in placing this photograph in such an early section.

While at the east end of the yard we notice that a vessel is just leaving. She is the 'King Edward VII' class battleship, *Africa*. Launched in the dockyard in 1905, she is now beginning to proceed down the river, having been commissioned on 6 November. With her upper deck lined by members of her crew, this is clearly a special occasion. Possibly it is the first time she has entered the Medway as a commissioned ship. A local photographer from the Chatham firm of Abrahams & Sons (117 High Street) is on hand to record the sight for posterity. Copies of this postcard were on sale throughout the Medway towns during the following week.

As we return to the main part of the yard we pass a number of older warships. These are the ships of the Reserve Fleet, held at the yard and ready to reinforce the Channel Squadron in the event of an emergency.

Among the ships in the Reserve Fleet is the ageing battleship *Camperdown*. In common with other vessels of this fleet, she has been stripped down to two-fifths of her normal complement.

Alongside the fitting-out basin a huge 160-ton crane stands ready to move some heavy items of equipment on board a warship that is approaching completion.

A peep into the No. 8 machine shop (adjoining No. 8 dock) gives an idea of the immensity of some of the buildings and the complexity of the machinery held within.

Outside No. 12 storehouse a small industrial steam engine named *Khartoum* prepares to take a variety of different ropes to a waiting warship.

At last we have entered the older part of the yard. In the distance can be seen the Admiral-Superintendent's house. He has overall responsibility for the dockyard and everything that occurs within. Appointed by the Board of Admiralty, he has this magnificent house to accommodate his family.

The destroyer *Greyhound* under repair in the No. 4 dock. This particular dock was originally timber built in 1685. At that time it was only 200 ft long. It remained little changed for well over a hundred years but by the late eighteenth century was frequently having to be repaired or improved. Finally, in 1836, work began on the task of rebuilding the dock in stone, while also taking the opportunity to both deepen and generally enlarge it. To the right of the dock stands the huge covering that was given to the No. 3 slip in 1838.

A splendid sight, as we continue to amble into the older part of the yard, is the No. 2 covered slip. This was first roofed in 1813. Since about 1880 it has been used as a store. Some fifty years after our tour it was to be destroyed in an accidental fire.

Taking a look into the colour-makers' shop, we catch a glimpse of some of the women members of the Chatham Dockyard workforce. They are engaged in the manufacture of flags for the Navy.

After an exhausting tour of the yard it is time to leave. The nearest point of exit is the Main Gate. Before reaching this we may glance briefly in the direction of the chapel. It has a naval cannon displayed at the head of its entrance pathway. The chapel was originally completed in 1808.

Having left the yard we take one final look back at the Main Gate. Because we have left sometime during normal working hours there are no crowds of workmen outside. Perhaps in an hour or so, this scene will be transformed. Hundreds of workers will pour out, all seeking the quickest way to their terraced homes in Chatham, Gillingham and Brompton.

SECTION THREE

Into the Medway

This section is devoted to a series of very special events that regularly took place at Chatham: the launch of a new warship into the Medway. Throughout its 414 years as a naval dockyard, over five hundred vessels were built at the yard, all of them receiving a ceremonial send-off. Each of these ships represented a great achievement on the part of those employed at the yard, and the occasion of the launch was marked out as a time for merriment and celebration. Those employed in building the vessel would be granted a half-day's holiday while hundreds of spectators would enter the yard to view the new ship as she slid down the launchway. To help create the right atmosphere, some of the buildings in the yard might be decorated with bunting and flags. As for the vessel, this at one time would have received huge flags and other florid additions to brighten up an otherwise colourless exterior. Finally, and ensuring that the day would be remembered by all those who attended, a band from the nearby marine barracks would open and close the ceremony.

Launch of the battleship *Agamemnon*, 17 September 1879. Although cameras were not unknown at this time, they lacked the sophistication necessary to record the vibrant activity to be witnessed when a ship was sent down the launchway. *Agamemnon* was built on the No. 7 slip, which had been roofed over in 1855. A great many people attended the launch, including two thousand invited guests who were given seats on a specially erected platform. Responsible for christening the vessel was Mrs W.H. Smith, wife of the then First Lord. Unfortunately, on this occasion, things did not go quite according to plan. The vessel, appearing to be about to move under her own weight, was sent into the Medway fifteen minutes early. Various boatmen, ready to assist in mooring her, were taken by surprise, with one boat caught immediately in her path. Those who could jumped out and swam to safety, but one of their number, a leadingman of labourers, was struck by the vessel and drowned.

A further engraving from the age of Queen Victoria shows the Chatham-built coastal defence ship *Glatton* lying alongside the dockyard wall. The crowd lining the dockyard and the vessel bedecked with huge flags confirms the date as 8 March 1871, the day of the vessel's first entry into the Medway.

Prince Rupert, following her floating out from the No. 2 dock, 12 March 1872. While a number of ships were built on slipways, the option always remained for a vessel to be built in dry dock. This happened when the vessel to be built was too large for an existing slipway or when all the slips were otherwise occupied. However, use of a dock was not normally favoured as it was an expensive facility that would then be unavailable for the docking of ships that were in need of repair.

The central battery ironclad *Alexandra* lies in the No. 1 basin towards the end of 1876. Launched at Chatham on 7 April 1875, she was originally laid down as *Superb*, but her launch by Princess Alexandra, the future queen, prompted a change of name. The presence of royalty at the dockyard meant that the yard was more lavishly decorated than might normally be the case, royal emblems emblazoning a great many of those buildings that overlooked the building slip. The vessel itself on the occasion of the launch was provided with an ornamental addition to her bows, consisting of a painted representation of the Prince of Wales' feathers.

The 'Majestic' class battleship *Magnificent* lies alongside the wall of No. 3 basin immediately prior to her departure from Chatham to join the Channel Squadron. A year has elapsed since her undocking, with the vessel having since entered the fitting-out basin where she received her machinery, ordnance and additions to her superstructure. When first launched, warships were nothing more than empty hulls that required much work before the ship might be regarded as complete.

The 'Formidable' class battleship *Irresistible* undergoes completion in the fitting-out basin, 1901. The vessel has yet to receive her main armament. She was launched by Princess Christian from the No. 7 slip on 15 December 1898.

Albemarle in the fitting-out basin, 1903. She was to be commissioned for the Mediterranean in November of that same year.

The 'London' class battleship *Prince of Wales* under construction in the No. 7 slip, 1901. She was to be launched by the Prince of Wales (the future Edward VII) on 25 March 1902.

Launch of the battleship *Africa*, 20 May 1905. *Africa* represented the first launching from No. 8 slip. This had been added to the yard a few years earlier and was much larger than any of the existing slips, which reflected the continued growth in the size of ships having to be built. Following this first launch, it became known as the 'Africa slip'. Unfortunately, despite the addition of this new facility, no further battleships were to be launched at Chatham. Instead, the dockyard developed a new specialism: that of constructing submarines. In this sequence of photographs, first issued as a commemorative postcard, *Africa* can be seen leaving the launchways, with the third in the sequence showing the vessel being towed round to the fitting-out basin by a paddle tug.

Launch of *Shannon*, 20 September 1906. For its day this is an excellent photograph of a cruiser being floated into the Medway. Note the diminutive size of flags compared with those used in the previous century. To ensure that a vessel the size of *Shannon* entered the Medway as smoothly as possible, the launchways had to be thoroughly greased. This involved the use of several tons of Russian tallow, over a hundred gallons of train oil and considerable quantities of soft soap. Once the vessel entered the Medway, huge amounts of tallow would float to the surface where it was collected by local boatmen. This is one reason why numerous boats were always present when a ship was launched.

A rare wartime photograph. The cruiser *Hawkins*, having been laid down on the No. 8 slip in June 1916, is now ready to be launched. It is possible that all those who had been involved in her construction are assembled for this commemorative photograph. The launch of this vessel took place on 1 October 1917.

The submarine HMS *Swordfish* on the verge of her launch into the River Medway. She was the thirtieth Chatham-built submarine and entered the Medway on 10 November 1931.

Swordfish moves down the launchway and into the River Medway.

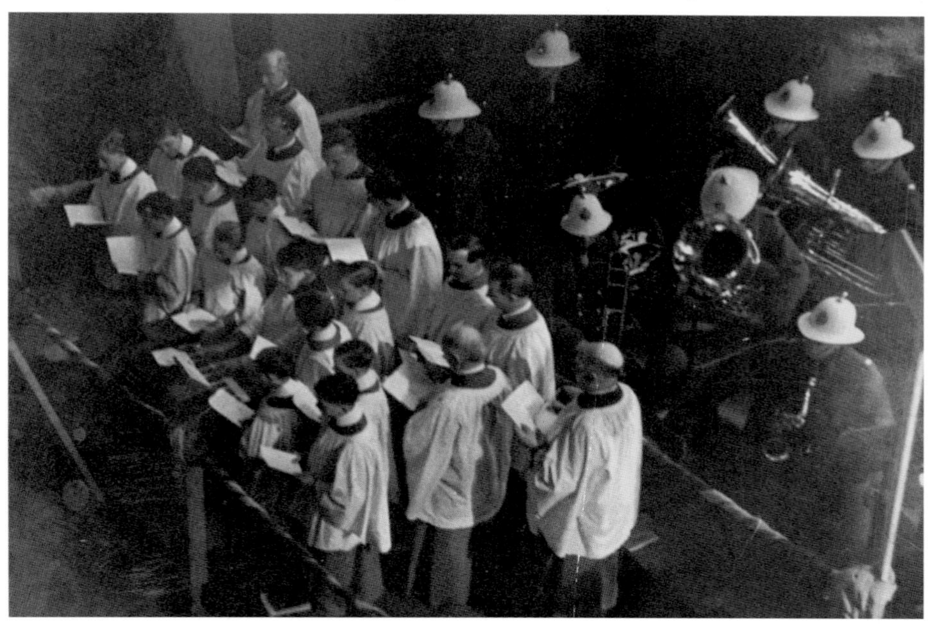

A choir, together with a Royal Marine band, inside the No. 7 slip during the launch ceremony of the Chatham-built submarine *Grampus*. The date is 25 February 1936.

Euryalus stands on the No. 8 slip ready to be launched. The poor quality of the photograph is easily explained. It comes from an ageing newspaper cutting that had been kept by one of the chargemen involved in building *Euryalus*. It was kept in his wallet for nearly fifty years and then loaned to dockyard historian Keith Slade for copying. That it had been kept for so long is ample proof of the pride with which those employed in the yard regarded their work.

The undocking of the 'Grimsby' class sloop *Deptford*, 5 February 1935. The fact that *Deptford* was fairly small and subject to being floated out of dock meant that there was only minimal local interest in this vessel when she made her first entry into the Medway.

A most unusual event was the simultaneous launching of two ships: *Modeste* and *Nereide*. Both were 'Black Swan' class sloops and laid down on 15 February 1943. This dual launch took place on 29 January 1944.

Final departure. The submarine *Tradewind*, launched in 1943, departs from the dockyard under naval colours. In fact, the vessel is at the mouth of the Medway, having left Chatham earlier that day. There can be no certainty as to the precise date of the photograph as *Tradewind* later returned to Chatham for a refit (1947) and subsequent modernization (1948).

Commemorative launch card issued for the christening ceremony of the survey vessel *Vidal*. She was the first survey ship to be equipped with a helicopter.

Although launched at Chatham in 1951, *Vidal* frequently returned there for regular refits. In March 1981 it became necessary to rebuild the bridge structure completely, a task undertaken inside one of the covered slips.

Oberon under construction in the No. 7 slip from where she was launched on 18 July 1959.

Spectators crowd under the roof of No. 7 slip to witness the launch of the 'Oberon' class submarine, *Ocelot*. Launched on 5 May 1962, she was the last warship to be built at Chatham for the British Navy. Three subsequent 'Oberons', *Ojibwa*, *Onondaga* and *Okanagan*, were built for the Canadian Navy.

Work proceeds on the first of the Canadian 'Oberons', HMCS *Ojibwa*. *Ojibwa* was launched on 29 February 1964.

The keel-laying ceremony for *Ojibwa* took place on 27 September 1962. This carefully posed shot shows two young ladies who had probably earlier presented a bouquet of flowers.

Okanagan descends the slipway of No. 7 slip, 17 September 1966. Built for the Canadian Navy she was the last warship launched at Chatham. Fears that the dockyard, without any further orders for construction, might be closed, were assuaged when it was decided that a nuclear refit centre would be built at the yard. As a result, Chatham developed one further specialism, that of refitting nuclear 'Fleet' class submarines.

A general view of the 'Africa' or No. 8 slip as it appeared during the 1970s. Following its construction at the turn of the century, all of the large surface vessels built at Chatham had been laid down on this particular slipway. Apart from *Africa*, *Shannon* and *Euryalus*, launches from this slip also included *Arethusa* (see Section Five). In more recent years, this whole area of the dockyard has been entirely transformed with virtually all of the buildings in view having been demolished.

Dock nos 2, 3 and 4. In earlier days, ships newly built in the dockyard would be brought into these docks for coppering of their hulls. This copper provided protection from the wood-boring mollusc known as shipworm. However, with the yard concentrating on iron shipbuilding together with the addition of the five docks around No. 1 basin, these docks were later used solely for general repair and maintenance work.

The dockyard's five covered slips. By the turn of the century, most of these had ceased to have any connection with shipbuilding, their huge enclosed spaces given over to storage. The exception, however, was slip No. 7 (furthest from the camera) which concentrated on submarine construction work.

SECTION FOUR

Of Might and Main

As can easily be imagined, the dockyard at Chatham was extremely busy throughout both world wars. While work continued on the construction of new warships, considerable thought also had to be given to the greatly expanded number of ships entering for repair, modification or refit. Nor did this increased workload represent an end to the tasks expected of those who worked at Chatham. Assistance had also to be given to the large number of shore bases that were established during both wars while the Second World War saw Chatham having to supply welding equipment for tanks and other fighting vehicles. On top of all this, there were inevitable delays to the progress of work as a result of threatened aerial attack.

During the First World War, the dockyard was a target for both Zeppelin airships and the ponderous Gotha bombers, while some twenty-five years later it was targeted by Stuka dive bombers and the less accurate Heinkel III. During autumn 1940 to fend off one such raid – or at least a formation of fifty bombers heading for London – the Chatham-built *Arethusa* opened fire with her 4-in anti-aircraft guns while in dry dock.

Female workers at Chatham Dockyard, from a photograph taken by Mr Cox of Gillingham in 1917. With the war in Europe having entered its third year, an increasing number of women were entering the yard, so allowing young men to join the fighting services. Usually, those leaving the yard were labourers or those in the lesser trades. On entering the yard, the newly recruited female workers were trained to undertake very specific tasks rather than the broad range normally acquired by an apprentice. On the extreme right of the group is a female chargehand while the only male present was probably responsible for training the women. In the front row (third from left) sits Constance Huggett, a crane driver. While names cannot be given to any other of the women, it is likely that most of them were employed in the No. 5 machine shop.

During the Second World War approximately two thousand women were employed in the yard. Among them was Constance Huggett, who returned to her earlier trade as a crane driver.

A major task undertaken at Chatham during the First World War was the preparation of ships for the Zeebrugge raid. This is *Vindictive*, a converted cruiser that was sunk at the entrance to Ostend harbour.

The United States armoured cruiser *Pittsburgh*, seen at Chatham towards the end of the First World War. Having been integrated into the Grand Fleet, American ships were regular visitors to the yard during this period.

As the First World War continued, Chatham found itself on the front line. The worst moment came on 17 September 1917 when four Gotha bombers attempted an attack on the dockyard. Loaded with 110-lb bombs, they failed to inflict any damage on the dockyard, but did rain havoc upon the surrounding area. In particular, one bomb hit the drill hall of the adjoining naval barracks, killing 136 ratings. This picture of the drill hall, taken from a contemporary postcard, was sent by a young recruit to a lady friend in Suffolk. He informed her that 'this is where the bomb dropped that time, right in the middle of that shed'.

R-3 passes St Mary's Island as she heads towards the mouth of the Medway. She was one of two 'R'-class submarines launched at Chatham on 8 June 1918, these being the last vessels to leave the launchways at Chatham prior to the end of hostilities. In all, twelve submarines and three light cruisers were launched at Chatham during the First World War.

Celebrating the end of war. This photograph was taken on 11 November 1918, Armistice Day, and shows how the yard had been specially decorated. Standing in front of a series of railway trucks are two members of the Metropolitan Police (Dockyard Division) together with a group of workers. To the rear stands a female employee, possibly a spinner from the nearby spinning floor. Unlike most of the women who had recently entered the yard, those employed on the spinning floor were not in fear of losing their jobs. Over the years, a tradition had emerged of employing spinners. However, a general reduction in yard numbers from a wartime peak of eleven thousand down to seven thousand eventually meant that even some of these workers found themselves threatened by redundancy.

The mould loft floor as seen in the 1920s. In the foreground a model of a 'C'-class cruiser can be seen while a mock-up of a submarine is located on the floor.

A particularly important vessel to be constructed at Chatham during the inter-war years was HMS *Kent*. The largest cruiser ever built in the yard, she was laid down in November 1924 and launched sixteen months later. In this picture, her forecastle deck is under construction while the ship's side frames and intermediate decks may be seen.

Further progress on the cruiser HMS *Kent*. Her upper deck beams have now been completed and deck plates are in hand. In the distance, the No. 5 machine shop is visible.

Kent in her war-time colours. Launched on 15 March 1926, she was initially commissioned as flagship of the 5th Cruiser Squadron.

Two destroyers lying side by side in dock No. 8. The two vessels, kept apart by shores, are chained together. This arrangement allowed maximum use to be made of facilities. It was a particularly common sight during the war years. However, this particular photograph was taken around 1932. Alongside the docks a crane appears to be under construction.

Wartime bomb damage. The No. 9 compressor house following an air raid in 1942.

The return of the 5,600 ton cruiser *Euryalus* to Chatham Dockyard. Launched from the No. 8 slip in 1939, *Euryalus* was the last cruiser to be built at Chatham. After leaving the dockyard in 1941 she served in the Mediterranean. By 1944 she had joined the Home Fleet and it was during this period of her service career that she returned to Chatham. Her 5.25-in guns are raised as if to fend off an aerial attack. In 1940, while being fitted out at the yard, she had been subjected to a number of bombing attacks and was clearly in a position to take retribution should another raid occur.

A further view of *Euryalus* upon her return to Chatham. Her aerial defences have been strengthened by the addition of a barrage balloon.

Officers of the Construction Division, *c.* 1945. They were the senior managers of the yard. During the Second World War they oversaw the laying down of 11 submarines, 4 sloops and 2 floating docks, as well as 1,360 refits.

SECTION FIVE

Arethusa

The building of *Arethusa* between 1933 and 1935 was an event of great importance for Chatham. In particular, it provided a large number of dockyard workers with guaranteed employment. More recently, those employed at the yard had become increasingly worried by the threat of unemployment. Indeed, many thousands had been laid off since the end of the First World War, with the possibility of even more following in their wake. These fears were always at their greatest on the launch or completion of a new warship, especially when there were few signs of the Admiralty appearing to place a new order. Since the launch of *Kent*, in 1926, the only new construction work directed to Chatham was that of a few sloops and submarines. A series of endless delays that seemed to suggest that the 1931 Naval Construction Programme, which included *Arethusa*, might never be implemented, had considerably heightened fears of future unemployment.

Only at the beginning of 1933 were these fears finally put to rest, the 5,220-ton cruiser finally being laid down on the No. 8 slip. A particular aspect of the new vessel was the use made of electric welding during her construction. The dockyard at Chatham had made only limited use of welding prior to this. Large numbers of shipwrights had to be trained in the new skills, as previously, as in other royal dockyards, warships had been riveted. The advantage of welding, however, was that it gave complete fixation while also reducing the overall weight of the vessel.

Laying of the keel plate, 25 January 1933. Invited to oversee this special ceremony was Lady Tyrwhitt, accompanied by her husband, Admiral Sir Reginald Tyrwhitt. The choice of Lady Tyrwhitt to officiate on this occasion was no random choice on the part of the Board of Admiralty. Her husband, who was then Commander-in-Chief of the Nore, had gained fame as captain of the last *Arethusa*. This vessel had ended her service career on striking a mine in 1916. However, in 1914 she had been Tyrwhitt's flagship at the Battle of Heligoland Bight. On that occasion she had engaged the German cruisers *Stettin* and *Frauenlob*. The assembled group at this keel-laying ceremony are warmly wrapped in a vain effort to keep out the biting chill of a severe east wind. As the keel plate fell into position, a Royal Marine band struck up 'A Life on the Ocean Wave'. Earlier, they had been playing a selection of Noel Coward numbers.

The keel of the future *Arethusa* was laid down on the No. 8 slip. This was the largest of the dockyard slips and the only one that had no roof. This aerial view shows the slip as it appeared shortly after the end of the Second World War. To one side are the dismantled plates from a 1,350-ton sloop. Owing to the cessation of hostilities, it had been decided to cancel any further work on this particular vessel.

Early stages in the construction of *Arethusa*. Work is under way on the outer bottom while the keel is still visible. The keel is held to the ground by hook and wire but once the weight of the ship has increased this arrangement will be unnecessary. In the foreground, lying on the after block, a mould (or pattern) is visible. This would have been made in the mould loft.

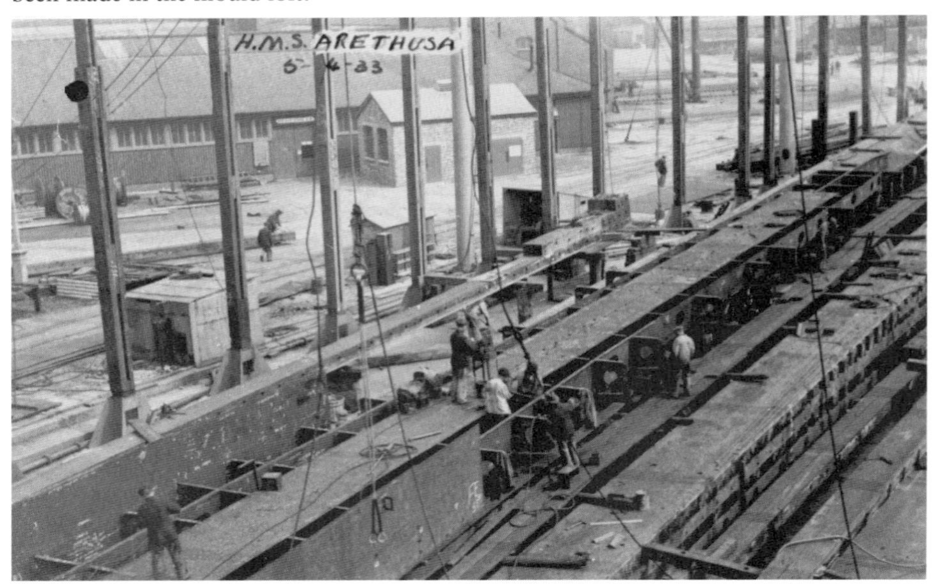

Progression of fore-end work. It is almost ten weeks since the keel plate was laid with the vertical keel also now in position. This stands upright to the outer keel and runs the entire length of the vessel. On top of the vertical keel are the gutter strakes.

Continued progress at the fore-end. Here, strengthening of the ship is of great importance for, as she nears completion, this part of the ship will house the magazines and barbettes. The photographer has chosen a similar view to that shown in the previous illustration and so allowing a direct comparison to be made. With this photograph taken on 5 May 1933, some fifteen to sixteen weeks have passed since the laying of the keel. As for the dockyard buildings in the background, the longer one is the No. 8 slip store while the smaller one is sub-station 'J'.

The port side after-end showing progress of construction. It is now 10 June 1933 (nineteen weeks since the keel was laid) and the shape of the vessel is beginning to be seen.

After-end and midship half of the ship. This photograph was also taken on 10 June 1933 and shows that considerable welding has been undertaken.

The hull is now complete and the superstructure erected on the upper deck. This is a clear sign that the launch is soon to take place. A further indication is that the dam at the end of the slipway is in the process of being removed.

Fore-end view of ship with launch cradles visible. This is a good view of the No. 8 slip as it shows the various assembled derricks. These were used to move various items of heavy equipment. The launch cradle is visible, appearing as a snug-fitting timber structure underneath the hull. Shortly before the launch the cradle would take the full weight of the vessel. It was designed to slide down the slip, the vessel sitting neatly in the cradle until it entered the River Medway.

A more general view of the ship as she lies on the slipway with the launch cradle in position.

One week before the launch. This picture could well have been taken on the same day as the previous two.

With the launch now imminent, water has been allowed to enter the slipway.

Launch day. On 6 March 1934, *Arethusa* was successfully launched into the River Medway. Prior to the official ceremony, members of the management team examine the bottle cradle at the bow of the ship. To save the embarrassment of the bottle failing to break, it was always carefully scored. Among this group are the foreman and construction manager. The foreman is wearing a bowler hat while J.E. Walker, the construction manager, stands immediately in front of him.

Arethusa enters the Medway. Invited to perform the naming and launch ceremony was Lady Tyrwhitt. She had previously overseen the keel laying. Crashing the bottle of wine against the bows, Lady Tyrwhitt was then handed a ceremonial chisel and mallet with which she severed a symbolic tethering rope. Then, in a very short time, the movement of the ship was expedited with the flag-bedecked vessel slipping into the River Medway.

Once launched, *Arethusa* was taken into the enclosed basins for fitting out. Here she would receive her machinery and other essential equipment. An important element of the No. 1 basin was the No. 9 dock, here seen sometime around 1938.

Arethusa was finally commissioned on 21 May 1935, joining the Mediterranean Fleet as flagship of the 3rd Cruiser Squadron. After a wartime career of mixed fortunes, she was eventually sold out of naval service and broken up in 1950.

SECTION SIX

Navy Days

Defence Secretary John Nott, in his June 1981 statement to the House of Commons, not only heralded the closure of Chatham Dockyard, but also served notice on the annual Medway spectacle of Navy Days. Both a public relations exercise and a means of collecting money for various naval charities, the last of these planned events was to have taken place in 1982. Unfortunately, a further event was to overtake even this last farewell, the entire programme being cancelled as a result of the Falklands crisis.

The tradition of annual dockyard open days was first established in the summer of 1928. With the Navy having recovered from the traumas of the First World War, the open day was seen as an ideal opportunity for the public to see the dockyard and visit some of those ships which had become household names. From then on, each passing year saw the idea developed and improved, with only the increasing likelihood of a second war with Germany forcing the dockyard authorities to seal its gates firmly on such an extravaganza. However, with Fascism firmly defeated, public displays were once again sanctioned, although the event itself was contracted from a Navy Week to that of Navy Days.

An advertising postcard for Navy Week, 1929. Apart from visiting forty assembled warships, those entering the dockyard on this occasion might view a field gun display, life saving by breeches buoy and the exciting re-enactment of the capture of an Arab dhow by the crew of HMS *Vindictive*. Nearly fifty thousand passed through the dockyard gates, each paying the princely sum of one shilling.

Cover of the sixpenny programme for Navy Week 1936. Displays that year included torpedo and depth charge firing and a submarine attack upon an armed merchant ship.

A scaled-down replica of an eighteenth-century warship that was specially built by Pembroke naval ratings for 1929 Navy Week. Modelled on HMS *Kent*, it was fully seaworthy and was put through its paces before an enthusiastic crowd.

Following the launch of the armoured cruiser *Kent* in 1926, a replica was also made of that vessel. However, it was not designed to float; instead the replica was placed on the chassis of a motor car. This allowed it to be driven around the streets of north Kent to advertise the fourth annual Navy Week that was held during August 1931.

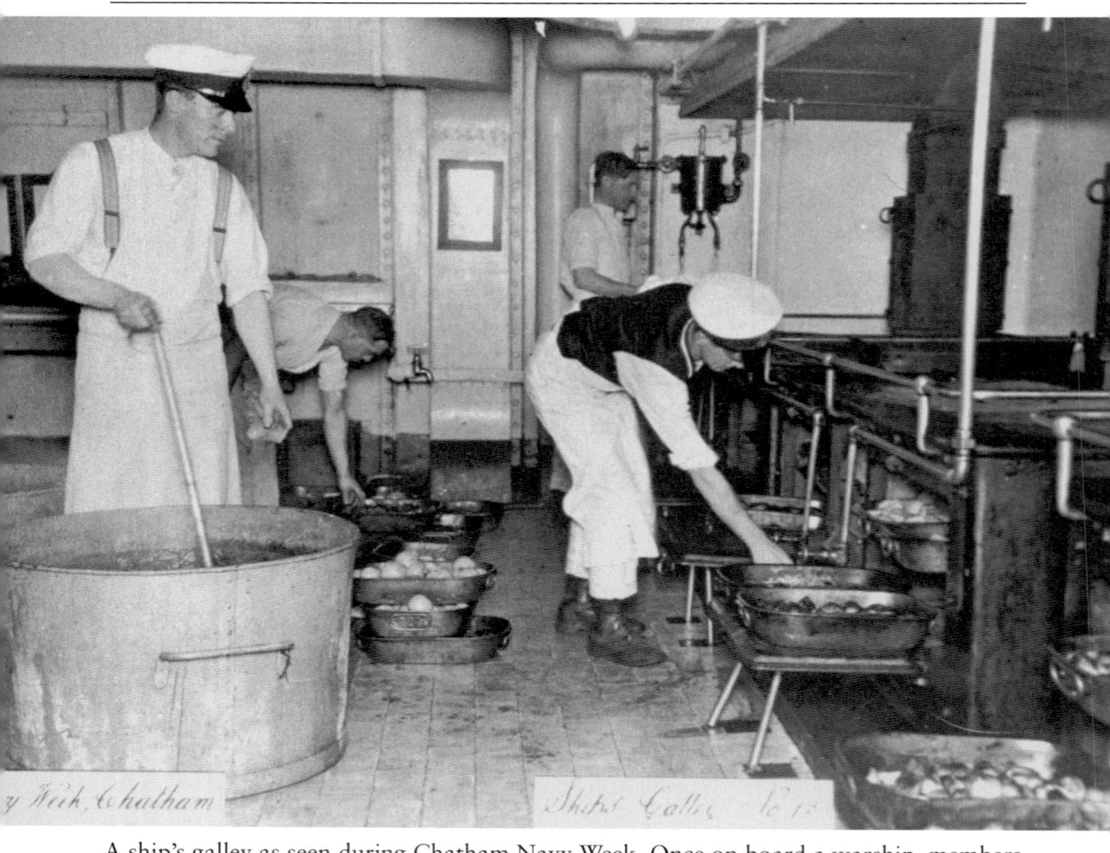

A ship's galley as seen during Chatham Navy Week. Once on board a warship, members of the public were encouraged to observe every aspect of naval life.

Another event that could be observed on board ship was the issue of grog. Both this and the previous photograph come from a set of fourteen postcards sold in the dockyard during Navy Week each year.

Naval divers who, during Navy Week, put on a display of open-sea diving in the North Lock. Remaining submerged at a depth of 120 ft, they had to carry 176 lb of additional weight.

Navy Days programme, 1952. By now the cover price had increased to 1*s* 6*d*. During the first Navy Week of 1928 forty ships had been open to the public, but by 1952 this had been reduced to six surface ships and four submarines. Admission to the event in that year was also 1*s* 6*d*. Unlike later years, cameras were not permitted, with special booths erected at each entrance to relieve visitors who had been ambitious enough to bring such a piece of apparatus. A nursery also existed, and families were allowed to leave their young children in the safe hands of Pembroke-based WRNS.

The cruiser *Superb* leaves No. 3 basin on 5 September 1952. During the previous month she had been the only cruiser present during Navy Days. Apart from smaller surface ships and submarines there were, of course, a number of special displays that included a fire-fighting demonstration, use of the breeches buoy and various static exhibitions.

A naval Wessex helicopter goes through its paces during a 1970s Navy Days. With crowds assembled round the No. 3 basin, the bows of HMS *Triumph* can also be glimpsed to one side of the picture.

One of the largest ships to be present in the last Navy Days events was the helicopter cruiser *Blake*. Laid down during the Second World War as a cruiser, she was converted in the late 1960s to carry Sea King helicopters. Again, she is seen entering the dockyard at Chatham.

One of the stars of Navy Days 1977 was the 'Leander' class frigate *Diomede*. She is seen here entering the yard through the south lock.

At the last of the Chatham Navy Days, held in May 1981, a number of ships from visiting navies were also present. Among those open to the public was the French Type 47 anti-submarine destroyer, FNS *Vauquelin*. This view of her stern shows that she is equipped with a Malafon anti-submarine torpedo launcher.

Another ship from a visiting navy present during 1981 Navy Days was the Belgian minesweeper, BNS *Antevelde*. She is seen in the No. 3 basin. Evidence that this part of the yard was built during the reign of Queen Victoria can be seen in the foreground.

Ships of the Standby Squadron seen during 1981 Navy Days. These vessels were not normally open to the public. However, their presence served as a reminder of an important task performed by the yard's workforce. These vessels, which were no longer in active service, were preserved at Chatham so that they might be ready for any sudden emergency. All vessels of the Standby Squadron received full above-deck maintenance while the below-deck areas were sealed to prevent corrosion. The vessels seen here are Type 81 general purpose frigates with HMS *Zulu* nearest to the edge of the basin. All these ships were scrapped when the yard was closed.

The last planned Navy Days at Chatham were to have taken place in May 1982. If it had gone ahead, this event would have been among the most ambitious of the post-war open days. Nineteen ships were to have been available for the public to visit, while plans also existed for a fly-past of piston-engined aircraft from the 1940s together with the then regular appearance of ship-board helicopters and Harrier jump jets.

SECTION SEVEN

Eve of Closure

Following the end of the Second World War, the dockyard at Chatham entered a long period of decline. At first this was characterized by a general reduction in the numbers employed together with less money available for the upkeep of buildings and other facilities. As the years went by, such cutbacks were accompanied by rumours of possible closure. Inevitably, these fears were dismissed by the government of the day. After all, the two local constituencies were both marginal seats and there was always the possibility that concern over closure might influence the way people chose to use their vote. These rumours reached a temporary peak during the early 1960s.

At that time, many of those employed at the yard were undertaking tasks connected with the new 'Oberon' submarines. But with only six having been ordered (three for the Royal Navy and three for the Royal Canadian Navy) and no other building work on the horizon, many felt that this confirmed their worst fears. It was only on the announcement that Chatham would be the site of a multimillion pound nuclear refit centre that the fear of closure, at that time, was finally allayed. Yet in the end, despite the completion of the refit centre, it was eventually decided that the yard should, in fact, close. This news reached the Medway towns in June 1981 following a government announcement in the House of Commons.

Chatham Dockyard, 1981. Running through the centre of this photograph are the three enclosed basins built during the nineteenth century. Nearest to the camera is the No. 1 basin with its five dry docks. The large warship that lies within this particular basin and adjacent to the Upnor wall is the helicopter cruiser, HMS *Blake*. Beyond the No. 1 basin can be seen the ships of the Standby Squadron which were all accommodated in the No. 2 basin. Finally, and disappearing out of the right-hand side of the photograph, is the No. 3 basin. Within this basin is the former aircraft carrier (then a heavy repair ship), HMS *Triumph*. Another feature worth noting is the Nuclear Refit Centre. This is easily identified as the buildings of the refit centre are dominated by the huge refuelling crane.

Rothesay, name ship of the 'Rothesay' class of frigates, undergoes a refit in the No. 9 dock. As with other ships of her class, *Rothesay* had recently joined the Chatham-based Standby Squadron.

The 'Leander' class frigate *Bacchante*, seen at Chatham during February 1977. She is in the process of being fitted with a gun which she was to transport to Gibraltar. At that time, the 'Leander' frigates were being brought to Chatham for conversion to Sea Wolf missiles.

The 'Leander' class frigate *Minerva* (F45) undergoes a major refit in the No. 9 dock during the 1970s.

The submarine *Opossum* (S19) undergoing a refit in No. 2 dock. Work on *Opossum* had begun in 1972.

The 'Leander' class frigate *Yarmouth* arrives at Chatham in 1972 to begin an eight-week repair programme because of damage to her bows. This damage was sustained during the Icelandic cod war, *Yarmouth* being the first Royal Navy warship to withdraw as a result of damage.

Construction work in progress on the Nuclear Refit Centre. It was eventually opened by Vice-Admiral Horace Law on 29 June 1968.

The main complex of the Nuclear Refit Centre was located between docks 6 and 7 and consisted of a refuelling crane, offices, workshops and a health physics building. However, the crane in this picture is one of two dockside cranes that stood either side of dock No. 6 while the tall building housed the offices necessary for administering the complex.

The health physics building. This housed the health physics branch which took responsibility for controlling radiological hazards that might result from the work of refuelling and refitting nuclear submarines. To undertake this task effectively, continual surveillance and frequent radiation surveys were carried out.

Workshops and refuelling crane. The refuelling crane was used for the placing of a portable workshop directly on to the submarine to allow fuel exchange to take place on board. During this process, the old uranium core was removed (for it contained fission products that reduced its efficiency) and replaced by a new core.

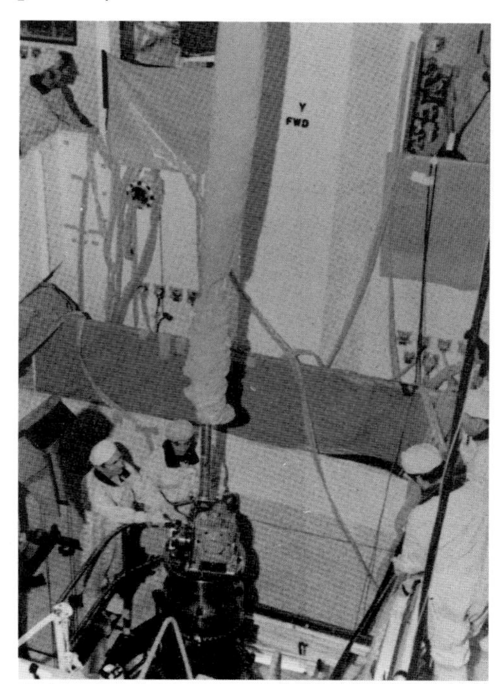

Dressed in protective clothing, refuelling branch team members are refuelling a nuclear submarine. The equipment is wrapped in plastic to keep it dust-free.

With work completed on the submarine HMS *Courageous*, a Royal Marine band was brought into the yard to help celebrate the occasion.

As the years rolled by, Chatham had become less of a male preserve. Among female workers employed within the Nuclear Refit Centre was Zandra Bradley, an electrical technician. Behind her, inside No. 6 dock, the submarine *Valiant* is coming to the end of her second major refit at Chatham.

Conqueror, a 'Fleet' class submarine, arrives at Chatham to begin a refit at the Nuclear Refit Centre.

The USS *Leader* in dry dock at Chatham. Beyond can be seen the refuelling crane towering above the Nuclear Refit Centre. Visits by US ships serving in European waters began during the First World War, as can be instanced by the picture of the USS *Pittsburgh* on page 60.

Moving back a few years and to a photograph of *Berry Head* in dry dock. Taken in 1959, it shows the vessel being prepared for a major refit. The extensive pile of gravel lying on the floor of the dock is ballast which had first to be removed from the vessel. *Berry Head* was a repair ship of 8,580 tons which had originally been built in Canada in 1944.

The ropery in 1963. Since the early nineteenth century women were regularly employed within the dockyard ropery. However, they rarely achieved equality with their male counterparts, usually being employed on a reduced day and for smaller wages. Furthermore, they had a separate entrance that gave them access to their work area. Here, a female employee is cutting fibres of manila hemp, the basic raw material for the manufacture of rope at that time.

The combed, cut and weighed manila fibres being automatically fed into waiting cans.

Under the frame of the ropemaking floor, 1963. An important task in the manufacture of rope was that of correctly reeving previously manufactured yarn through register plates. These plates were uniformly perforated and separated the yarn so that it formed correctly when twisted into strands.

Annual drawing office conference held at Chatham Dockyard, *c.* 1981, and attended by senior managers of all naval dockyard drawing offices. The drawing office at Chatham (part of the design division) supplied working drawings for most departments in the yard. In particular, the drawing office would be heavily involved at the outset of any planned refit. Among those from Chatham are Alan Kettle, general manager of the dockyard (seated, centre) and Keith Slade, then the newly appointed drawing office manager, seated second from right. Despite its closure, Keith Slade has retained an overriding interest in the yard, and is an undoubted expert on its history. Many of the photographs included here have come from his personal collection.

The launch of a new caisson. Caissons, or floating gates, are used at the entrance to dry docks to ensure that no water can enter once it has been pumped dry. Vessels held in dry dock can have work undertaken on the lower part of their hulls, with water allowed to re-enter the dock only when the vessel is due to be returned to the Medway. On 15 December 1954, the caisson at the entrance to No. 3 dock gave way, allowing river water to enter. At the time, the submarine *Talent* was undergoing repair. As a result, she was carried across the Medway where she grounded on a mud bank. Tragically, the accident resulted in four dockyard workers losing their lives. Following the accident, it was decided that all caissons should be replaced. The caisson in the photograph is awaiting launch, with a further one having already passed down the slipway.

One of the new caissons under construction, 22 January 1962.

The completed No. 5 caisson awaits her launch, 14 December 1962.

The completed No. 7 caisson lying in the partially flooded No. 9 dock is to be floated out on completion, 23 March 1964. Another caisson lies in the foreground.

One of the new caissons, having been placed at the mouth of a dock, is under test. The dock is flooding as if a ship which had completed a repair programme is about to be floated out.

Electrical department open day, 1960. Used to demonstrate the work of electrician apprentices in the yard, the open day was designed to allow parents of apprentices to view the work they had carried out during the year. This photograph was loaned by Mrs Field, daughter of Cyril Cates, a lecturer in the department who helped set up the display.

As recognition for long service in the yard, dockyard employees were presented with special medals. Among those presented with a long service medal in 1975 was Nelson Holden. The group is assembled in front of the Admiral's office with Mr Holden seated immediately to the right of Rear-Admiral S.F. Berthon, Admiral-Superintendent of the yard.

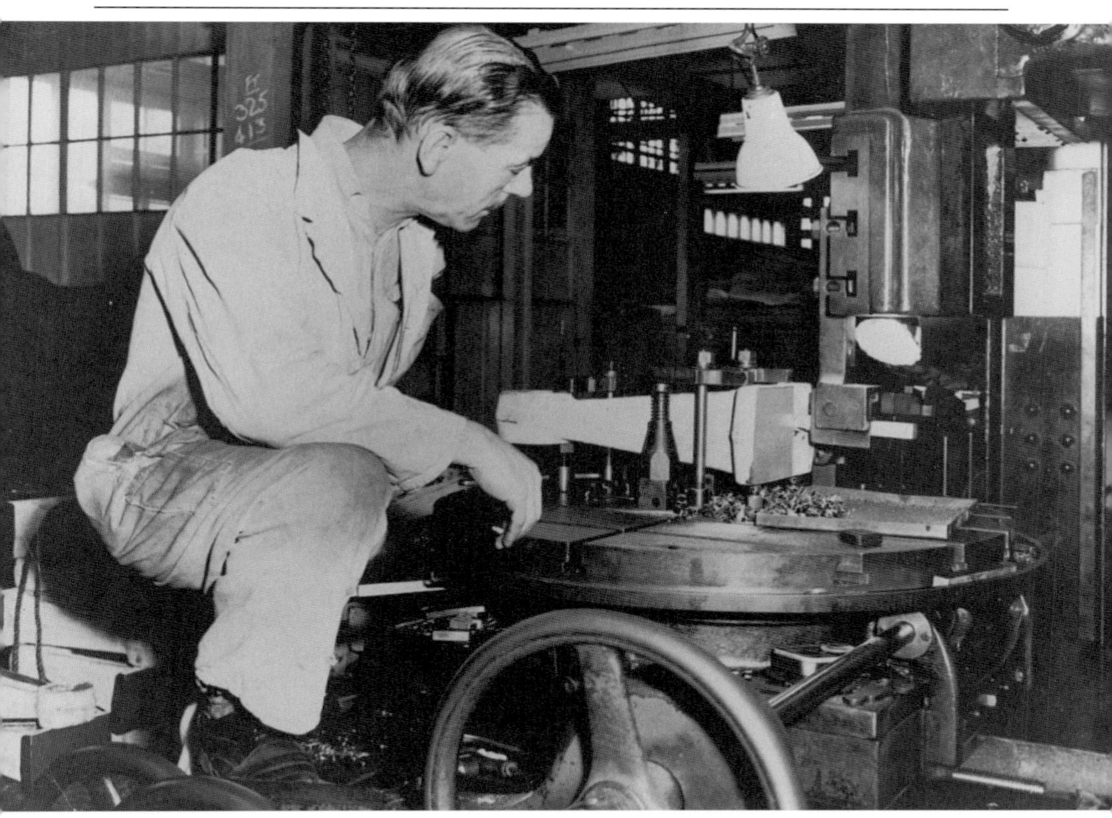

Nelson Holden at work in the yard in March 1965. He is seen alongside a vertical shaping machine that he operated. This was in use for the manufacture of piston rods that were to be fitted to the engines of the new 'Oberon' class submarines. Mr Holden first entered the dockyard in 1929 as a yard boy in the ropery. With Nelson as his given name and his birthday on Trafalgar Day, it seems natural that he should serve in the dockyard that built HMS *Victory*.

In 1977 the Ministry of Defence Police (who had taken over responsibility for dockyard security in 1971) acquired their first river launch. This was specially adapted in the boathouse. Among those who worked on it was Colin Bolton, then a shipwright, who is standing to the left of this group. The policeman in the foreground is Superintendent Arthur Salter, head of the Chatham Dockyard force.

Sgt Henry Bentley, a member of the Ministry of Defence Police. Apart from dockyard security, members of this police force undertook all normal policing duties, including traffic control, investigation of accidents and even care of lost property.

Fibreglassing the fire-damaged figurehead of HMS *Nelson*. This once stood outside the No. 2 covered slip and was damaged during the same fire that destroyed this particular slip. While there could be no question of saving the figurehead itself, the fibreglassed head was partially restored and presented to the local fire brigade. Undertaking the work is Colin Bolton, who had previously worked on the prefabrication of the superstructure moulds for 'Oberon' submarines. As an economy and time-saving measure, these submarines incorporated layered fibreglass.

In November 1977 Prince Philip visited the dockyard and is here seen being presented to the dockyard trade union representatives. Nearest to the camera is Bill Stevens (senior negotiator for non-industrial workers) while beyond are John Mustoo and Jack White. Rear-Admiral Berthon stands with Prince Philip.

HRH Prince Charles during his visit to the naval base and dockyard in June 1980.

Logs arriving at the dockyard sawmill, May 1975. The sawmill stood on St Mary's Island and was responsible not only for sawing and re-sawing timbers required for the various departments in the dockyard at Chatham, but also undertook considerable amounts of work for the naval dockyards at Rosyth and Portsmouth. On first arriving, these logs would be stored behind the sawmill before being cut into more manageable sizes known as fliches. A later re-sawing could see these fliches then cut to specific sizes required by the ordering departments.

An English oak log being cut into fliches. The saw has been temporarily stopped while wedges are pushed into the timber so as to prevent the blade becoming trapped. George Warren stands in the foreground with Alan Elphick beyond.

Joe Sawkins oversees the cutting of English elm into a keel or transom for boat building by one of two Stenner re-saws. In the background stands the supervisor, Harry Lowry.

Members of the personnel department, 1976. Among those on the back row are Fred Nicholson, welfare officer, and Jim Rowland (second and third from left respectively); Eileen Griffin and Bert Foulser (fifth and sixth from left); John Bubb (eighth from left). Seated (left to right) are Den Cornish, Gerry Lodge, Ray Alexander, Phil Beaumont and Harry Hewson. It was Eileen Griffin, a secretary at the time, who loaned me this photograph. She has many fond memories of the dockyard in the years that led up to its closure. Those in the personnel department were a close-knit community who not only supported each other but rarely missed the opportunity to play practical jokes on each other. Certainly Eileen was particularly sad when the dockyard closed, although by that time she had been transferred to London.

'Get yer skates on.' One of the jokes played was on Freddy Matthews who temporarily held the post of combined personnel and management and product services manager. Always rushing around, he was presented with these joke skates made by some of the apprentices at the yard.

On moving to the naval dockyard at Devonport, Ray Alexander, personnel manager, was presented with an amusing leaving card that was spiced with jokes and carried the motif 'Alexander the Great'.

The dockyard telephone exchange, *c.* 1960. While the dockyard was a manufacturing centre, employing hundreds of skilled and semi-skilled workers, it also employed a sizeable white-collar staff. The telephone exchange stood behind the officers' terrace and next to the dockyard wall.

Jim Lewis, vice-chairman of the industrial trades union representatives, receiving the award of a British Empire Medal from Sir Anthony Buck (then under-secretary of state, Royal Navy).

Dockyard trade union representatives seen at their farewell party on the eve of the yard's closure in March 1984.

Secure jobs at the dockyard! An advertising hoarding at Gillingham Football Ground proclaims the advantage of working at Chatham Dockyard. It was erected shortly before the closure announcement.

SECTION EIGHT

Under New Management

On 1 April 1984 the area of the former naval dockyard came into the possession of three separate bodies: Chatham Historic Dockyard Trust, English Estates and Medway Dock Company. Each was responsible for a different area of the former dockyard and each had an entirely different objective. The oldest part of the yard, the area beyond the Main Gate, was entrusted to the Chatham Historic Dockyard Trust. This organization, using the numerous historic buildings within this area, had as its objective the creation of a living museum. Because of the poor state of a large number of these same buildings, much thought and effort had initially to be directed to repair, maintenance and restoration. But English Estates, which acquired the Nos 2 and 3 basins together with a large area of the adjoining land, had a completely different task. Instead of creating a tourist attraction, English Estates had to concentrate on the need for job creation. Finally, Medway Dock Company, having already acquired the No. 3 basin, had the task of developing commercial port facilities.

The galvanizing shop shortly before closure of the yard in 1984. This is one of many buildings that has since seen a total transformation, now serving as the 'Visitor Centre' for those wishing to tour the historic part of the yard. Instead of the industrial machinery it once housed, the galvanizing shop now contains a bookshop, numerous artefacts relating to the yard, a model of the yard and an audio-visual room.

When the dockyard first closed there was a great deal of work to be undertaken, not least tidying the various hidden-away corners that had suffered many years of neglect. Among such corners was the old chain cable shed store that used ancient cannons to support its sloping roof.

An important element of the yard's history is its association with HMS *Victory*. This plaque, lost since the closure of the yard, once stood at the head of No. 2 dock. It tells of how Nelson's famous flagship was built and floated out from this dock.

Soon after acquiring control of the dockyard, the Chatham Historic Dockyard Trust decided to transform the eighteenth-century Upper Mast House into a permanent exhibition centre that shows how a wooden warship was constructed. In preparing the exhibition, not only had the building to be completely renovated but exterior fire-proof cladding had to be removed in order to reveal the original timberwork.

Transformation. The Upper Mast House shortly after the opening of the 'Wooden Walls' permanent exhibition.

Late eighteenth-century timber sheds. Built at a time when huge amounts of newly delivered timber was wasted as a result of poor storage, these sheds provided protection from the elements while allowing the free circulation of air. Their more recent restoration was carried out with help from the government-funded agency, English Heritage.

The nineteenth-century naval sloop *Gannet* undergoes restoration in the No. 3 dock. Built at the former naval dockyard of Sheerness, she was brought to Chatham in 1987. It is intended that the vessel will be restored to her original appearance and placed on permanent display.

September 1993, and progress on *Gannet* continues. Partially coppered, she has also been fitted with a specially commissioned gannet figurehead.

Another vessel undergoing restoration prior to being placed on public display is the submarine *Ocelot*. Unlike *Gannet*, she was actually built at Chatham, launched from the No. 7 slip in May 1962.

An aerial view of that part of the dockyard redeveloped by English Estates. In the foreground is the old repairing basin which is now surrounded by a series of office buildings while towards the centre may be noted the work site of the Medway Tunnel. Also to be seen are the covered slips of the historic dockyard together with the North Mast Pond.

Among companies that have been attracted to the commercial port at Chatham is Kent Line. Here, one of their ro-ro vessels, the *Duke of Anglia*, can be seen inside the No. 3 basin.

A solitary reminder of the many Victorian factory buildings that previously existed within the area of the nineteenth-century extension is the machine shop that still stands close to the No. 1 basin. Once a covered slip, it was in use at Woolwich Dockyard until the closure of that particular yard in 1869. It was subsequently brought to Chatham and re-erected in 1880.

Included in the redevelopment of the former dockyard is an important road network that links with a tunnel carrying traffic under the River Medway. In June 1994, when this picture was taken, work was under way on the tunnel approach road. An area of the dockyard once dominated by worksheds and machine shops, little now exists that would suggest the presence of a major naval dockyard on this site.

A visitor to Chatham Maritime in June 1994 was the American 'Liberty' ship, USS *Jeremiah O'Brien*. Brought to the area of the former dockyard to commemorate the yard's connection with D-Day, the *Jeremiah O'Brien* herself saw active service during the invasion of Europe. Open to the public, she received many thousands of visitors during her short stay.

Acknowledgements

I would like to thank the following people who kindly loaned photographs for inclusion in this book: Mr Colin Bolton, Mrs Sylvia Field, Mr David Gomar, Mr Nelson Holden, Mrs Kathleen Lowry and Linda Mower. In addition, the Royal Engineers Library (Brompton Barracks) and English Estates have also helped with photographs. However, a particular thank you must be reserved for the Chatham Dockyard Historical Society who allowed me to reproduce a number of photographs from their extensive collection.

A further special thank you must also be reserved for both Keith Slade and Harold Bennett. Keith Slade not only helped with a great many photographs but also proved a mine of information on developments in the dockyard during the nineteenth and twentieth centuries. For his part, Harold Bennett, as chairman of the Chatham Dockyard Historical Society, put a great deal of time aside to guide me through the society's collection.